Journey of Hope

The Birth of the Savior

A MUSICAL BY

Camp Kirkland & Tom Fettke

lillenas
PUBLISHING COMPANY
Lillenas.com

Creative Presentation Options

for

Journey of Hope

1. JOURNEY OF HOPE is a complete concert work performed as is. If you wish, appropriate Christmas carols could be added between the sections to involve the audience.

2. Since JOURNEY OF HOPE is arranged in the sequence of the Christmas story, appropriate scriptural narrations or responsive readings may be inserted at the beginning of each section. For example:

Part II	Isaiah 7:14
Part III	Isaiah 9:2, 6; Matthew 12:21
Part IV	Luke 2:1-4
Part V	Luke 2:6-7
Part VI	Luke 2:8-14
Part VII	Reading provided in the body of the work
Part VIII	Options: Luke 1:46b-47; 1:68; Ephesians 1:3.
Part IX	2 Corinthians 8:9
Part X	Psalm 98:4, 7-9

3. You may wish to illustrate the various Christmas events presented in JOURNEY OF HOPE by use of multi-media (particularly slides) and/or tableau (a depiction of the scenes in an area of the stage by silent and motionless costumed participants, with or without scrim lighting).

4. JOURNEY OF HOPE can become a full-blown musical drama by adding dramatic scenes between the sections.

5. Use portions of JOURNEY OF HOPE in your own concert, pageant, or living Christmas tree.

6. Each section is designed to stand alone if you wish. Each may be presented as a Sunday morning anthem during the Advent season or utilized at other special events where the choir may participate; i.e., a candlelight carol service or Christmas eve service.

7. INVITATION OPPORTUNITY Although it is optional, we hope everyone will elect to use this moment in the musical for spiritual renewal and outreach.

8. PASTORAL CONCLUSION The theme of JOURNEY OF HOPE is a great set-up for the new millennium. As we face an unknown future, There Is Hope! That hope is communicated clearly in this work, with passion and power. Thus after "The Lord Will Come Again", you may wish your pastor to conclude the presentation with a few words of encouragement. The benediction, "There Is Hope", would follow. If the Pastor utilized the Invitation Opportunity for his short closing message, you may wish to end the presentation in a bright and triumphant mood. Thus "The Lord Will Come Again" would be the last selection. Or go directly to "There Is Hope - Benediction" after "The Lord Will Come Again" (or after a closing prayer).

9. The overture may be used as a postlude.

Contents

Part I
JOURNEY OF HOPE
Overture

includes
Adoration
O Come, All Ye Faithful

Arranged by Camp Kirkland
and Tom Fettke

*"Adoration"

CD: 1 Warmly, rubato ♩ = ca. 80

18
rit.
*"O Come, All Ye Faithful"
23
Bright ♩= ca. 128
mf
27
tr
31
35
B♭
F

2nd time to Coda
(to pg. 8, meas. 60)

Cm/F
B♭M7/F
Ped.
D.S. al Coda
(to pg. 6, meas. 23)
57
B♭M7/F
E♭m6/F
CODA
N.C.
62
C♭
Fm7
67
N.C.
ff
B♭
C/B♭
B♭
rit.
C/B♭
B♭
C/B♭
B♭
8vb

Part II

THE JOURNEY BEGINS

includes

Emmanuel– Prince of Peace
His Name Is Called Emmanuel
Emmanuel

Arranged by Camp Kirkland
and Tom Fettke

Majestic ♩ = ca. 84

*Words and Music by Camp Kirkland and Tom Fettke.

*Words by Ken Bible and Tom Fettke; Music, Plainsong, adapt. by Thomas Helmore.

19
won - der - ful than words can tell.
19
CM7
Em/B
Am6
B sus
B m
Em2
23
Born in our dark - ness, He is
Em/D
23
Am/C
Bm7
Am7
Bm7
C
26
CD: 4
Light. Born in our weak - ness, He is
26
D sus
D/C
C2(no 3rd)
Bm7
Em
Em7
Am7
Bm/D
D

Divisi f
29
might. Em - man - u - el, Em -
G sus G D/F♯ Em Bm/D
man - u - el. His name is called Em -
33 decresc.
Am/C Am7 B B7/D♯ Em Em/D CM7 G6/B G/B
Faster ♩ = ca. 128
36
rit.
man - u - el.
Am Em/B Bm7 C
mf

*Words and Music by Michael W. Smith. © 1983 Meadowgreen Music Company (ASCAP). All rights administered by EMI Christian Music Publishing. Used by permission.

46
man - u - el, Em - man - u -
Fm6/C
C
el.
50
Won-der-ful Coun-sel - or,
F Em7 Am
Em7 Am G
Divisi
Lord of life, Lord of all.
CD: 8 3rd time
54
He is the Prince of Peace, Might-y God
F/G

CD: 6
Ho - ly One.
Em - man - u -
Am B♭
B♭M7 C/B♭ B♭ C/B♭
58
el,
Em - man - u - el.
(to pg. 13, meas. 42)
Unison mp
Em -
Am Am/G FM7 Gsus G C
2
Em - man - u - el,
Em - man - u - el.
B♭ A Dm C/E F B♭ A

64
CD: 7
Dm C F E Am G/B C
Unison mp
(to pg. 13, meas. 42)
3
69
Em - Em - man - u -
C Bb C/Bb Bb M7 C/Bb Bb C/Bb
el, Em - man - u - el,
Am Am/G F M7 G sus G Am Am/G F M7

73
cresc.
Em - man - u - el,
Em - man - u -
Gsus G Am Am/G FM7 Gsus G
el.
77
fff
Em - man - u - el.
A♭ Gm7 N.C.
Fm6/C C Fm6/C C Fm6/C C
8va
8vb

Part III

JOURNEY OF HOPE

includes

There Is Hope

O Little Town of Bethlehem

Arranged by Camp Kirkland
and Tom Fettke

11
Divisi
cresc. poco a poco
dark to re - veal the light of Hope gives our spir - its
Am Dm7 Gsus G C CM7 Dm/C C
peace, peace breaks forth in praise for the prom - ised
Gsus G G/F C2/E C/E C/G FM7
15
King for His gift of grace, God's most Ho - ly
G Em7 E7sus Em7 FM7 Dm7 Dm6 Dm7

One, Yet our hearts cry out 'til Mes - si - ah
E7 E7♯5 E7 Am FM7 F6 FM7
f
comes. We be - lieve tho' we face de - spair. For
19
Gsus G/F C2/E C/E F C G/B Am Fm6/A♭
CD: 10
still there is hope.
C/G Gsus G C A♭/C

24
Unison
mf
Hope ech - oes thro' the day, Thro' a fer - vent
Unison mf
D♭ G♭/D♭ D♭ A♭sus A♭ A♭/G♭
27
prayer, voic - es speak from faith, wor - ship fills the
D♭2/F D♭/F G♭M7 A♭ F7♭9/A F7/A
30
Divisi
air. God re-veals His love and Hope gives our spir - its
Divisi
B♭m E♭m7 A♭sus A♭ D♭ D♭M7 E♭m/D♭ D♭

cresc. poco a poco
peace, peace breaks forth in praise for the Prom - ised
Ab sus Ab Ab/Gb Db2/F Db/F Db/Ab GbM7
King, for His gift of grace, God's most Ho - ly
34
Ab Fm7 F7sus Fm7 GbM7 Ebm7 Ebm6 Ebm7
One. Yet our hearts cry out 'til Mes - si - ah
F7 F7#5 F7 Bbm GbM7 Gb6 GbM7

CD: 11
ff rit.
comes.
39 Unison f a tempo
Hope gives our spir-its
A♭sus A♭ B♭sus B♭ E♭ A♭/E♭ E♭
cresc. poco a poco
peace, peace breaks forth in praise for the Prom - ised
B♭sus B♭ B♭/A♭ E♭/G E♭/B♭ A♭M7
42
Divisi
King, for His gift of grace, God's most Ho - ly
B♭ Gm7 G7sus Gm7 A♭M7 Fm7 Fm6 Fm7

44
One. Yet our hearts cry out 'til Mes - si - ah
G7 G7♯5 G7 Cm A♭M7 A♭6 A♭M7
ff
comes.
48
f
We be-lieve,
B♭sus B♭/A♭ E♭2/G E♭/G A♭
decresc.
tho' we face de-spair. For still there is hope, for
mf
E♭ B♭/D Cm A♭m6/C♭ E♭/B♭ F/A

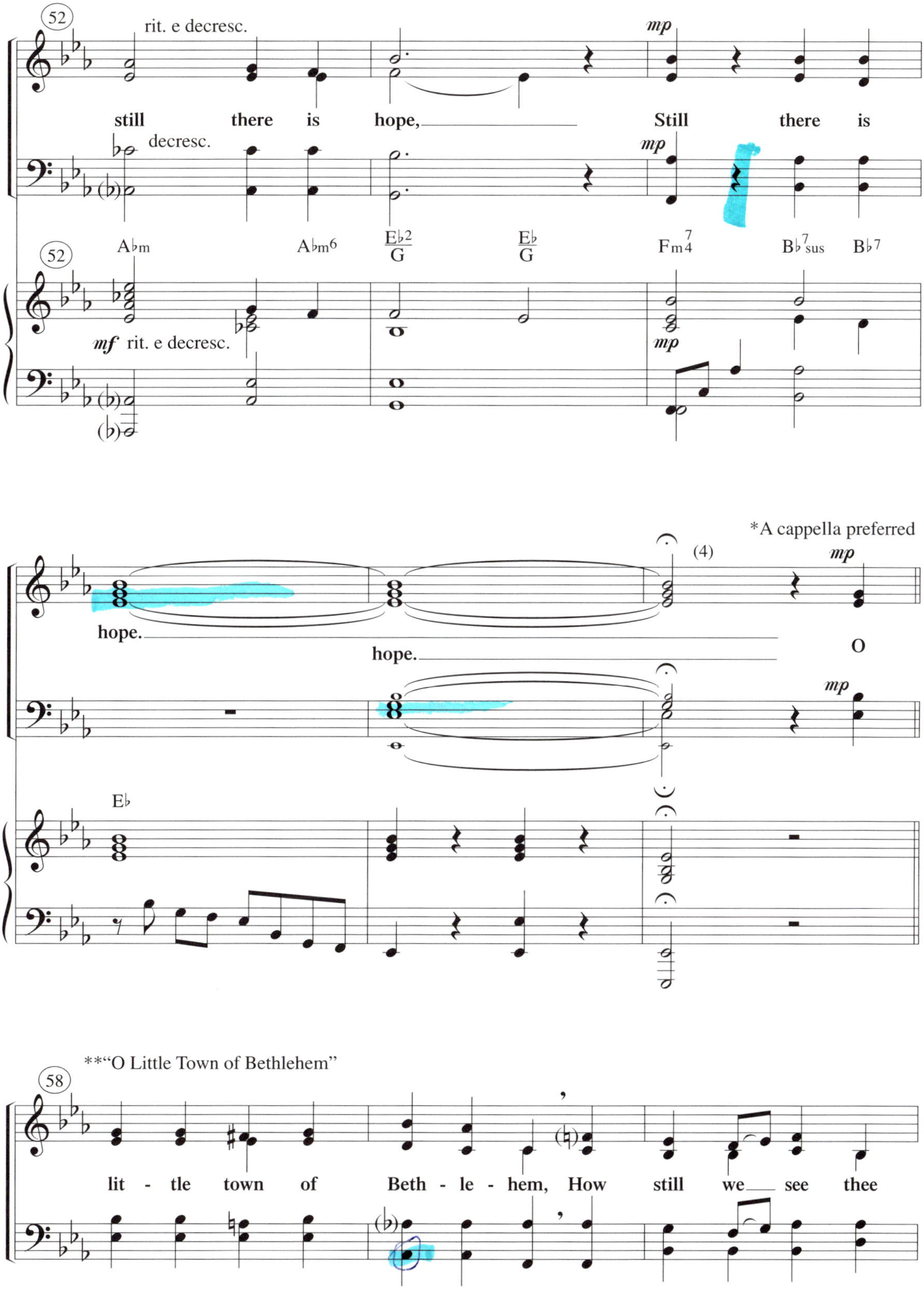

*No accompaniment is provided on the accompaniment trax. If support is need, a live keyboard(s) may be used.
**Words by Phillips Brooks; Music by Lewis H. Redner. Arr. © 1999 by Pilot Point Music (ASCAP). All rights reserved. Administered by The Copyright Company, 40 Music Square East, Nashville, TN 37203.

62
lie! A - bove thy deep and dream - less sleep The
66
si - lent stars go by. Yet in thy dark streets
shin - eth The ev - er - last - ing Light; The
70
hopes and fears of all the years Are
met in thee to - night.

Part IV

JOURNEY TO BETHLEHEM

includes

On a Silent Christmas Night

Hope Has Arrived

Arranged by Camp Kirkland and Tom Fettke

*Words and Music by Christopher Machen. Administered by The Copyright Company, 40 Music Square East, Nashville, TN 37203.

13
young man and his bride to be would lodge there for the night.
A(no 3rd)
Bm2
17
Why this town of strang - ers?
Men unison (or male solo) mp
Bm
A
17
D2
21
What had God be - gun? And why did He choose
Divisi
Bm
A
G
21
Em7
A
A
G

CD: 13
Beth - le - hem for the birth - place of His Son?
Unison
D/F♯ Bm7 Em7 Em9 A G/A Bm
Divisi mf
26
On a si - lent Christ - mas night, In an
Bm DM7/A G A A/C♯ D D/C♯
mf
30
or - di - nar - y place, Where the world would hard - ly no -
Bm Asus A Em

- tice there came a mir - a - cle of grace. And a
D/F♯ Esus D C Asus A A/G D/F♯
34
vir - gin would give birth, And a star would shine its light;
G A A/C♯ D Bm DM7/A
38
For her Child would save the sons of earth on a
G A/G D/F♯ Bm A/B Bm

CD: 14
si - lent Christ - mas night.
Em7 D/E A7sus A7 G/A D A/C♯ Bm7
43
f
Unison
Beth - le - hem! Tho' you are small in - deed,
A A/G G A/G D/F♯
From you would come a King for
A7sus/E D 47 G2 D2/F♯ D/F♯

Divisi
51
all e - ter - ni - ty. He will rise
Divisi
Em7
Asus
A
51
a Shep - herd to His sheep.
Unison
Unison
A/G
G/G
A/G
D/F♯
A/E
B/D♯
55
CD: 15
1st time
decresc. 2nd time
He will be great, this One will be our
decresc. 2nd time
55
Em7
Esus
Em7
D/F♯
Bm7
C2
decresc. 2nd time

(to pg. 31, meas. 43)
60
mf
peace.
peace,
He
will
Asus
A
Em7
Em9
rit.
Faster 𝅗𝅥 = ca. 80
be
our
peace.
G/A
B♭
mp
64
E♭
E♭2 4
CD: 16
68

*Words and Music by Rebecca J. Peck.

84
giv - en To res - cue
dark - ness We share the
Ab/C Cm7 Fm7 Eb/G
all man - kind.
hope of Christ.
Fm/Ab Cm/A Bbsus Bb
88
Divisi
f
Tell - ing forth the great an - nounce - ment,
Like the an - gels, we pro - claim it
Ab Bb Ab AbM7 Bb
An - gels loud - ly sing - ing,
With our joy - ous sing - ing,
Fm7 Eb/G Ab Eb/Bb Bbsus Bb

92
"Born this day is Christ, the Sav - ior,"
Tell - ing all the won - drous mes - sage,
A♭ B♭ A♭ A♭M7 B♭
CD: 17 1st time
CD: 19 2nd time
Hear the mes - sage they are bring - ing.
Hear the good news we are bring - ing.
Fm7 E♭/G A♭ A♭M7 F/A A♭6/B♭ B♭sus
98
Hope has ar - rived, He's
B♭ B♭/D E♭ E♭sus E♭ Gm7 E♭/G
102
Unison
ly - ing in a man - ger. Love is fast a -
A♭ B♭/A♭ A♭ A♭M7 B♭ B♭/D E♭ B♭ B♭/D

sleep on the hay. In a
E♭ B♭ E♭2/C B♭/D B♭
106
tin - y ba - by boy, peace and
Divisi
E♭ B♭/D E♭ B♭/D
joy have come;
C m7 G m7 A♭
111
CD: 20 2nd time
Hope has ar - rived,
B♭/A♭ A♭ E♭/G
CD: 18 1st time
He's God's on - ly Son, His on -
1 Son.
E♭/G F m7 A♭/B♭ B♭7 E♭2 4 E♭ E♭2 4

(to pg. 34, meas. 72)
116
Unison mf
- ly Son.
2.We who
E♭2 4
E♭
Choir unison
mf
120
2
Son.
Ev - ery long - ing
E♭
B♭/F
G♭
in the heart of man
Has
D♭2/F
124
been ful - filled with - in Him.
D♭m/F♭
A♭/E♭

128
He's peace in our trou - ble,
A♭/E♭ A♭/D♭ E/B
132
CD: 21
cresc.
joy in our strug - gles, Hope to start
G♭/D♭ A♭/E♭
cresc.
o - ver a - gain.
E♭ E♭/D♭ C sus C
136
Ladies only (Divisi)
f
Hope has ar - rived, He's ly - ing in a
F F sus F A m7 F/A B♭ B♭ B♭M7
f

140
Unison
man - ger. Love is fast a - sleep on the
C C/E F C C/E F
hay. In a tin - y ba - by
144
C F2/D C/E C F
Divisi
boy, peace and joy have
C/E F C/E Dm7 Am7
149
come; Hope has ar-rived, He's
B♭ C/B♭ B♭ F/A

153
God's on - ly Son. Hope has ar-rived,
Gm7 B♭/C C7 Dm Dm/C B°7
He's God's on - ly
F/C C7sus B♭/C C7
157
Son, His Son,
Son, His on - ly Son, Son, His on -
F4 2 F F4 2 F F4 2 F F4 2
His Son, God's Son.
- ly Son, Son, His on - ly Son.
F4 2 F F4 2 F F4 2 C7 F

Part V
JOURNEY TO THE MANGER

includes
Heaven's Child
Child in the Manger

Arranged by Camp Kirkland
and Tom Fettke

*Words and Music by Joel Lindsey.

warm Him from the cold, hard - ly what she pic - tured in the
sang Him to sleep, but they mar - veled at the prom - is - es this
F/C C C/E F C2/E
12
proph - e - cies of old, It seemed al - most im - pos - si - ble to
ba - by came to keep, His Fa - ther must have felt at once great
B♭ F2/A G7sus G7 F2 F G2 G
CD: 23 1st time
CD: 25 2nd time
think it could be true, But as she pon - dered in her heart she
sad - ness and great joy As He watched His lit - tle ba - by
C C/B Am Dm7 Dm7 4 C2/E C/E

rit.
16
a tempo
knew.
boy.
This was Heav - en's Child
this was Heav - en's Child,
Choir
mp
Oo
Heav - en's Child,
mp
G sus
G
G13
G7
C
D/C
rit.
a tempo
In an earth - en sta - ble, wrapped in glo - ry, meek and mild.
Oo
F
C2/E
B♭
F2/A
G7sus
G7

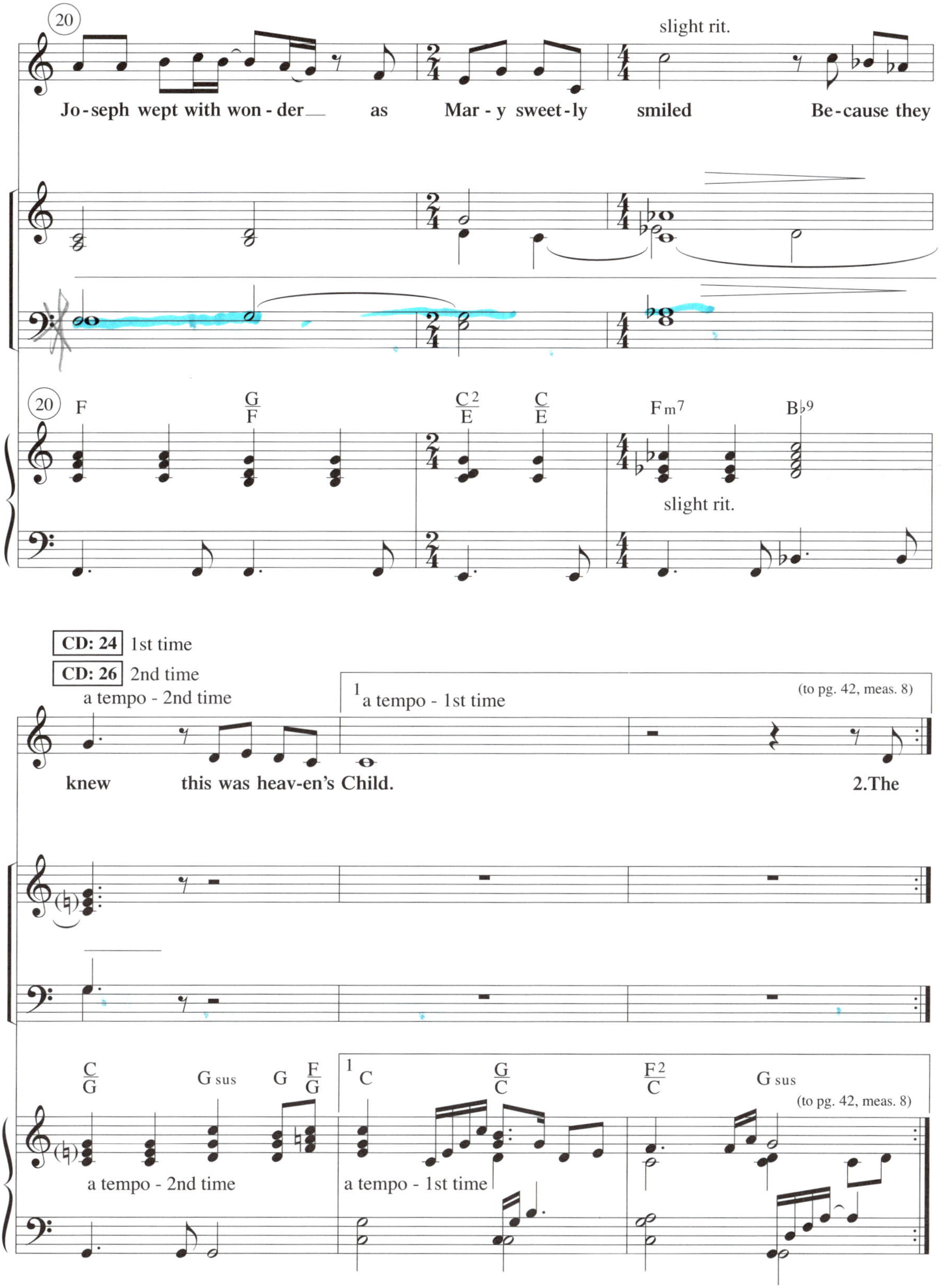
20
slight rit.
Jo-seph wept with won-der as Mar-y sweet-ly smiled Be-cause they
F
G/F
C2/E
C/E
Fm7
B♭9
slight rit.
CD: 24 1st time
CD: 26 2nd time
a tempo - 2nd time
1 a tempo - 1st time
(to pg. 42, meas. 8)
knew this was heav-en's Child. 2.The
C/G
G sus
G
F/G
C
G/C
F2/C
G sus
a tempo - 2nd time
a tempo - 1st time

27
mf
Child.
Mar - y's lit - tle ba - by boy was
Ah
C
G
B
Am
Em7
Jo - seph's pride and joy,
Still they wished the world would see that
Ah
Dm7
Am
FM7
Dm6
F
Em7
Am7

rit.
He was so much more.
rit.
Unison
This was
Unison
F
G
Em7
A7sus
A7
A13
A7
rit.
32
a tempo
Heav - en's Child,
Heav - en's Child
a tempo
Heav - en's Child,
this was
Heav - en's Child.
32
D
E
D
a tempo

In an earth - en sta - ble, wrapped in glo - ry, meek and mild.
Oo
G
D2/F♯
C
G2/B
A7sus
A7
36
Jo-seph wept with won - der as Mar - y sweet - ly smiled
Divisi
Divisi
G
A/G
D2/F♯
D/F♯
Gm7
C9

40
CD: 27
grad. rit.
decresc.
Unison
mp
Be - cause they knew this was Heav - en's Child,
C9 C13 Gm6/B♭ D2/A G6/A A7 Bm7
mp grad. rit. and decresc.
Be - cause they knew this was Heav - en's
44
Gm7 C13 C9 D/A A/B Bm7 Em7 Em7/A

a tempo
rit.
Child.
p
This was Heav-en's Child, this was Heav-en's Child
D
E
D
a tempo
rit.
48
This was Heav - en's Child.
(6)
pp
Heav - en's Child.
Gm6
D
D2
D
8vb

*Words by Ken Bible and Mary MacDonald; Music by Thomas J. Williams, Camp Kirkland and Tom Fettke. Copyright © 1999 by Pilot Point Music (ASCAP). All rights reserved. Administered by The Copyright Company, 40 Music Square East, Nashville, TN 37203. Tune EBENEZER used by permission of of Eluned Crump and Dilys Evans.

71
Ho - ly Child of high - est Heav - en,
Men unison
mf
Dm
C/D
Dm
C/D
Dm C/D Dm
75
CD: 29
Yet on Him our sins will
Dm C/D
Dm C/D Dm
C/D Dm C/D
79
Divisi f
fall. Al - le - lu - ia!
f
Divisi
Dm
Dm/C
B♭
F/A
Fsus/G
F
f

83
Al - le - lu - ia! Al - le -
Gm/E A7/C♯ Dm
83
B♭ F/A
lu - ia, Christ the Lord.
Fsus/G F F/C C
87
Ho - ly Child of high - est
87
B♭ F/A Fsus/G F Gm/E A7/C♯

91
Heav - en. Al - le - lu - ia,
Dm
B♭
C/B♭
F/A
B♭
CD: 30
Christ the Lord.
F/C
C7sus
C7
F
B/D♯
98
Unison mf
Proph - ets fore -
Unison mf
Em
C
D
D/F♯
Em
Em/D
C
mf

102
told Him, In - fant of Won - der, An - gels have
D Em B Em/C♯ B7/D♯ Em B7 Em Am
sung His praise a - bove.
106
Hear them
Hear them,
Em B7 Em/B B Em
Divisi
fill the earth with mus - ic,
the earth,
110
CD: 31
God has
For
B/D♯ Em/D CM7 B Em B Em Am

cresc.
come in peace and love.
cresc.
Em
Em/B
B
Em
Em/D
cresc.
114
f
Al - le - lu - ia! Al - le -
C
G/B
Gsus/A
G
Am/F♯
B7/D♯
lu - ia! Al - le - lu - ia,
118
Em
C
G/B
Gsus/A
G

122
Christ the Lord. Hear them
G/D D C G/B
fill the earth with mus - ic,
G sus/A G A m/F♯ B 7/D♯ E m
126
CD: 32
Al - le - lu - ia, Christ the
C D/C G/B C G/D D 7sus D 7

131
Lord. Al - (Al) - le -
G G 4 2 G/B C/F
131
D♭ A♭/C
lu - ia! Al - le - lu - ia!
A♭sus/B♭ A♭ B♭m/G C7/E Fm
135
Al - le - lu - ia, Christ the
135
D♭ A♭/C A♭sus/B♭ A♭ A♭/E♭

139
Lord. Hear them fill the
E♭ D♭ A♭/C A♭sus/B♭ A♭
CD: 34 2nd time
1 CD: 33
earth with mus - ic, Al - le -
B♭m/G C7/E Fm D♭ E♭/D♭
(to pg. 58, meas. 131)
lu - ia, Christ the Lord.
A♭/C D♭ A♭/E♭ E♭7sus E♭7 A♭
(to pg. 58, meas. 131)

2
Al - le - lu - ia!
D♭
E♭/D♭
A♭/C
D♭
150
Al - le - lu - ia!
153
Al - le -
D♭
E♭/D♭
A♭/C
D♭
E♭/D♭
156
lu - ia,
Christ
the
A♭/C
D♭
D♭/C
B♭m7
E♭7sus
E♭7

160
Lord! He is the Lord!
A♭ F♭ G♭ A♭
He is the Lord! Christ is the
A♭ F♭ G♭ A♭ F♭ G♭
164
Lord!
A♭ F♭ G♭ A♭

Part VI

JOURNEY OF THE SHEPHERDS

includes

Gloria in Excelsis Deo
Angels, from the Realms of Glory
Angels We Have Heard on High
Glory to God in the Highest

Arranged by Camp Kirkland
and Tom Fettke

*Words and Music by Camp Kirkland and Tom Fettke.

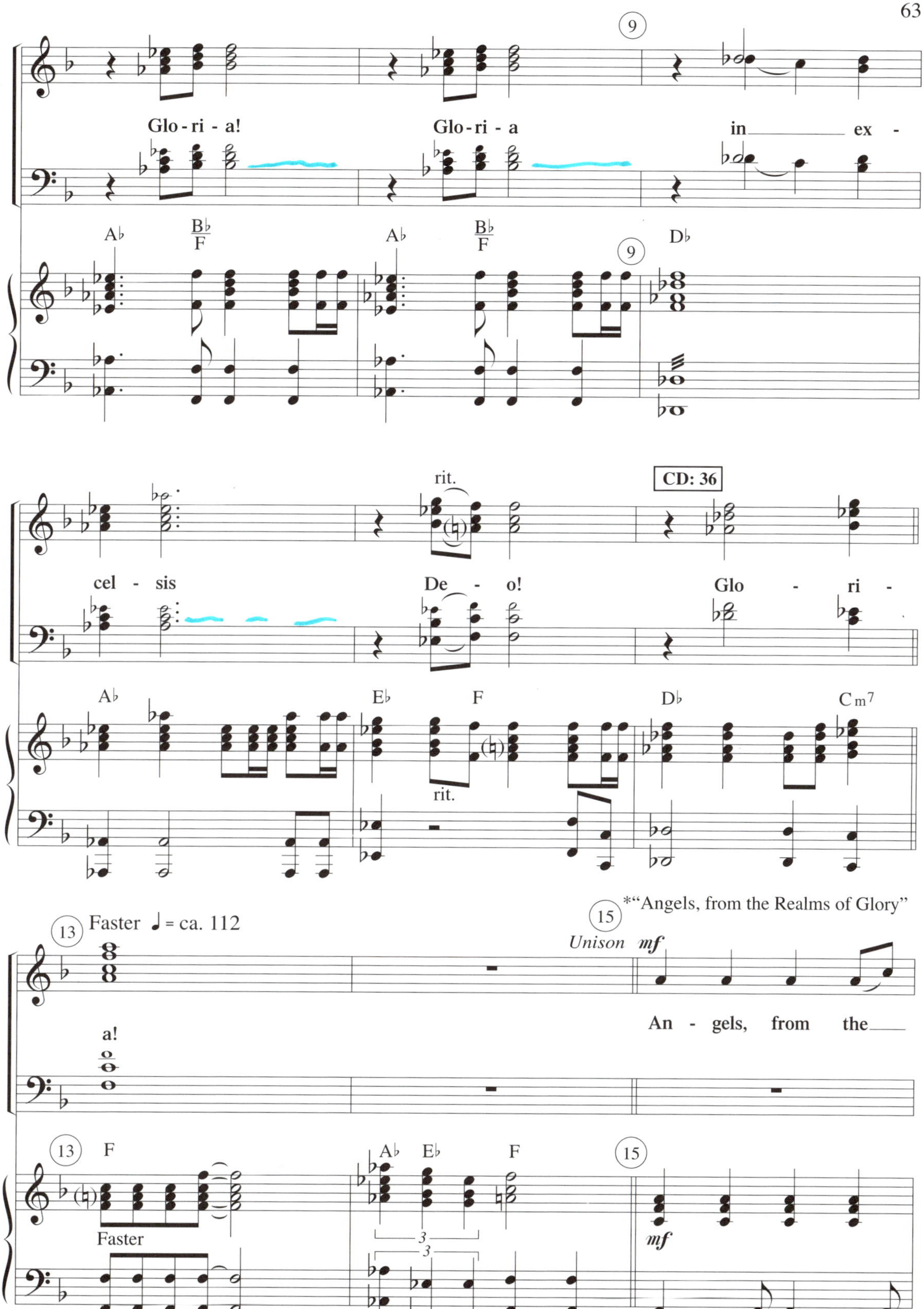

*Words by James Montgomery; Music, Traditional French Melody. Arr. Administered by The Copyright Company, 40 Music Square East, Nashville, TN 37203.

realms of glo - ry, Wing your flight o'er all the earth.
C/E F Dm Dm/C B♭2 F/C A/C♯
19
CD: 37
Unison mf
Ye who sang cre - a - tion's sto - ry, Now pro - claim Mes -
Dm Am7 Gm4 7 F/C A 7♯5/C♯ Dm Dm/C
23
Divisi f
Come
si - ah's birth. Come, O come. Come, O come.
Gm4 7 C F Am7 D 7♯5 Gm7 C7

and wor - ship
Come, O come, wor - ship
Christ the new - born
Divisi
F B♭6 C F C/E Dm B♭m/D♭
King.
29
Come
Come, O come. Come, O come.
Unison
F/C C 29 Am7 D7♯5 Gm7 C7
and wor - ship
Come, O come, wor - ship
33
Wor - ship Christ the
Divisi
F B♭6 C 33 F C/E Dm B♭m/D♭

CD: 38 1st time
CD: 40 2nd time
2nd time to Coda
new - born King.
2nd time to Coda
F/C C7sus C7 F C F A♭ E♭ F
37
Unison
mf
Shep - herds, in the fields a - bid - ing, Watch - ing o'er your flocks by night,
37
FM7 E♭M7 Dm7 B♭M7
mf
41
Unison mf
CD: 39
God with man is now re - sid - ing;
41
Dm Dm/C B♭ F/A

*Words, Traditional French Carol; Music, Traditional French Melody. Arr. © 1999 by Pilot Point Music (ASCAP). Administered by The Copyright Company, 40 Music Square East, Nashville, TN 37203.

53
De - o! Glo - ri - a, glo - ri - a,
Glo - - -
Unison
G/D D G E7 Am D7
glo - ri - a, glo - ri - a!
- - - ri - a!
Divisi
57
In ex - cel - sis
G C Am7 D G D/F♯ Em Cm/E♭
De - o, In ex - cel - sis De - o,
G/D D7 Em G/F C2/E Cm/E♭

61
molto rit.
Faster ♩ = ca. 92
In ex - cel - sis De - o!
G D/F♯ Em Cm/E♭ G/D D7 G
molto rit.
Faster
CD: 41
G N.C. G G♭
67
Men's trio (or double trio)
Solo mf
"Look
F E♭ B♭ F
mf

*Words and Music by Daryl Williams.

CD: 42
83
heav-en-ly host a - round the throne joined in to
F
Dm
F/C
C7
say:
87
"Glo - ry to God in the high - est, peace on earth
F
and good will to men." Heav-en-ly an - gels an-nounced His ar -
91
F
Gm/C
F
ri - val in the lit-tle town of Beth - le - hem. Hal - le-lu -
Dm
G9
C7
Gm7/C
C7

95
- jah to the Lord sing ho - ly; He was born___ to save the world_ from
F
Gm/C
F/C
99
sin. Glo - ry to God in the high - est, glo - ry ha - le - lu -
F
CD: 43
- jah to the Lord, A - men.
F
C7
F
D7
C/D

104
f
"Glo - ry to God in the high - est, peace on earth and good will to
Choir
mf
"Glo - ry to God, Peace and good
mf
104
G
Am/D
f
men." Heav-en-ly an - gels an-nounced His ar - ri - val in the lit-tle
will," Heav'n - ly an - gels,
G
108
Em

112
town of Beth - le - hem. Hal - le - lu - jah to the Lord sing
town of Beth - le - hem. Hal - le -
A9 D7 Am7/D D7 112 G
ho - ly; He was born to save the world from sin. Glo - ry to
lu - jah, save the world from sin.
G Am/G G/D G

116
CD: 44
God in the high - est, glo - ry ha - le - lu - jah to the Lord, A -
Glo - ry to God, to the Lord, A -
G
G/D
D7
men.
1st tenor
121
"Glo - ry to
men.
2nd tenor
Sing "Glo - ry to God in the high - est,
men.
Baritone
"Glo - ry to God in the
men.
"Glo - ry to
G
C/D
G

God in the high - est, peace, good will to men."
glo - ry, peace on earth, and good will to men." Heav - en - ly an -
high - est, peace on earth, good will to men."
God, Peace and good will,"
G
Am/D
G
125
An - gels an - nounced His ar - ri - val in the town of
- gels an - nounced His ar - ri - val in the lit - tle town of Beth - le -
An - gels an - nounced His ar - ri - val in the town of
Heav'n - ly an - gels, town of
G
Em
A9

129
Beth - le - hem. Glo - ry, sing, hal - le - lu - jah,
hem. Hal - le - lu - jah to the Lord, sing ho - ly; He was born
Beth - le - hem. Hal - le - lu - jah, sing - in',
129
Beth - le - hem. Hal - le - lu - jah,
D7 Am7/D D7 129 G
133
CD: 45
He will save from sin. Glo - ry to
to save the world from sin. Glo - ry to God in the high - est,
He will save from sin. Glo - ry to God in the
133
save the world from sin. Glo - ry to
G Am/D G/D G 133

God in the high - est, hal - le - lu - jah to the Lord, A -
glo - ry, hal - le - lu - jah to the Lord, A - men!
high - est, hal - le - lu - jah to the Lord, A -
God, to the Lord, A - men.
G
G/D
D7
G
C/G
men!
"Glo - ry to God in the high - est,
ff
Sing "Glo - ry to God in the high - est, glo - ry, peace on earth,
ff
men!
"Glo - ry to God in the high - est,
138
f
"Glo - ry to God,
f
E♭7
138
A♭
ff

142
peace, good will to men." An - gels an -
— and good will to — men." Heav - en - ly an - gels an - nounced His ar -
peace on earth, good will to men." An - gels an -
142
Peace and good will," Heav'n - ly
A♭ B♭m/E♭ A♭
142
nounced His ar - ri - val in the town of Beth - le - hem.
ri - val in — the lit - tle town of Beth - le - hem. Hal - le - lu -
nounced His ar - ri - val — in the town of Beth - le - hem.
an - gels, town of Beth - le - hem.
Fm B♭9 E♭7 B♭m7/E♭ E♭7

146
Glo - ry, sing, hal - le - lu - jah, He will
- jah to the Lord, sing ho - ly; He was born to save the world from
Hal - le - lu - jah, sing - in', He will
146
Hal - le - lu - jah, save the world from
146
A♭
B♭m/E♭
A♭/E♭
CD: 46
150
save from sin. Glo - ry to God in the high - est,
sin. Glo - ry to God in the high - est, glo - ry, hal - le - lu -
save from sin. Glo - ry to God in the high - est,
150
sin. Glo - ry to God, to the
A♭
150

154
hal - le - lu - jah to the Lord, A - men!
- jah to the Lord, A - men! Hal - le - lu -
hal - le - lu - jah to the Lord, A - men!
154
Lord, A - men.
A♭/E♭ E♭7 A♭ D♭/E♭ 154 A♭
Glo - ry, sing, hal - le - lu - jah, He will
- jah to the Lord, sing ho - ly; He was born to save the world from
Hal - le - lu - jah, sing - in', He will
Hal - le - lu - jah, save the world from
A♭ B♭m/E♭ A♭/E♭

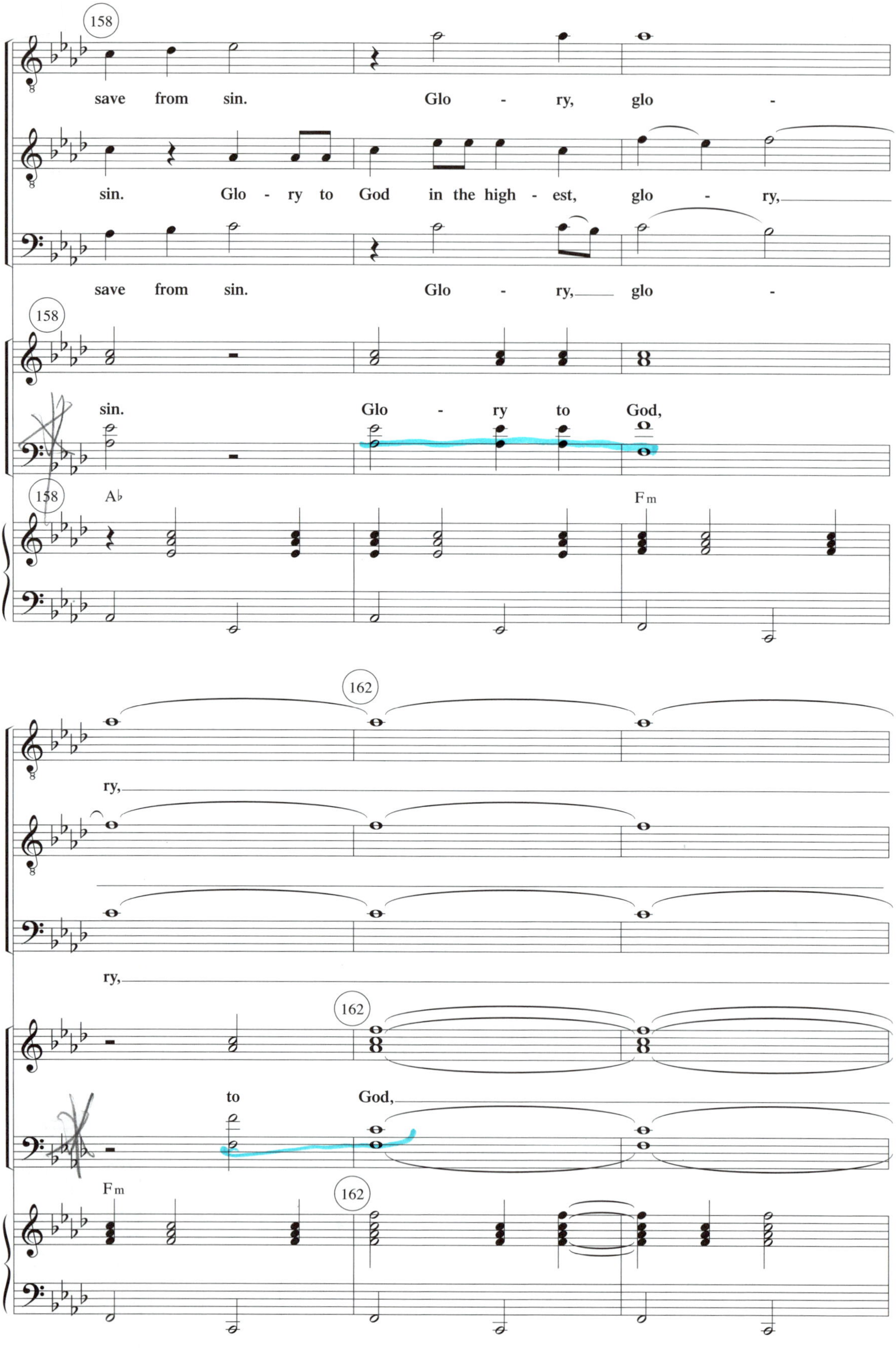

158
save from sin. Glo - ry, glo - ry,
sin. Glo - ry to God in the high - est, glo - ry,
save from sin. Glo - ry, glo - ry,
sin. Glo - ry to God, to God,
A♭
Fm
162

166
A - men!
hal - le - lu - jah to the Lord,
hal - le - lu - jah to the Lord,
Hal - le - lu - jah,
Fm
A♭/E♭
E♭7
A♭
(8)
A - men!
A - - - men!
A - men!
A♭
E♭
A♭

Part VII

JOURNEY OF SIMEON

includes

He Is Emmanuel

My Eyes Have Seen Your Salvation

Arranged by Camp Kirkland and Tom Fettke

*"He Is Emmanuel"

With conviction ♩ = ca. 66

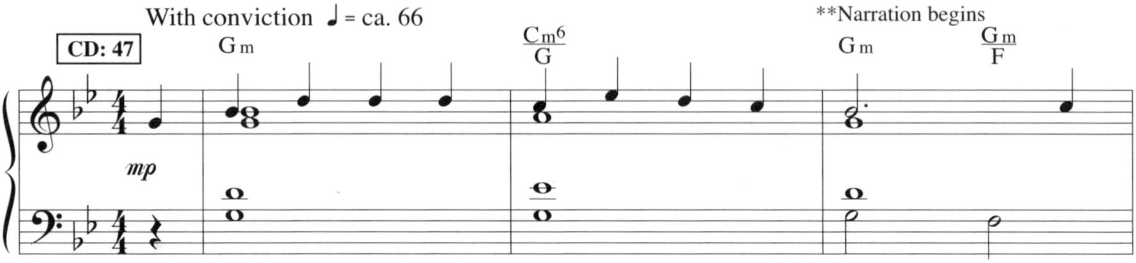

**NARRATOR: Four hundred years had passed since a great prophet had spoken God's Word to the people.

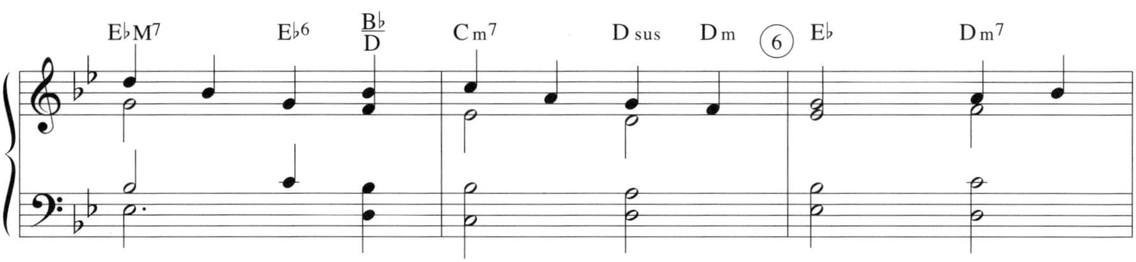

The Romans ruled and oppressed Israel, and yet the people held a deep longing and tenacious hope that surely…some day…in some way…a

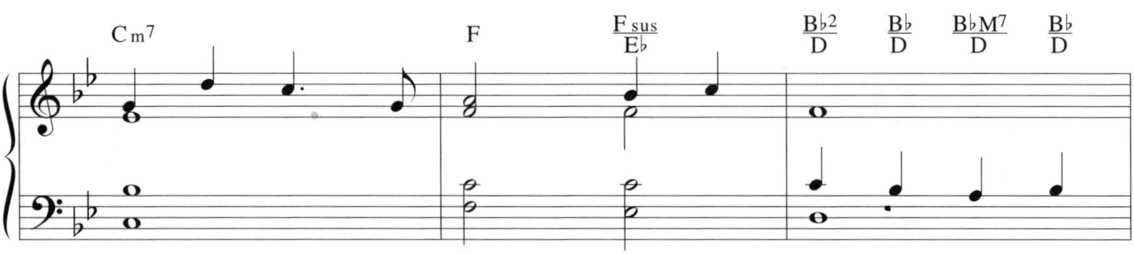

silent God would speak again. The Scriptures tell us that at this time there was a man in Jerusalem who had such hope. His name was

Simeon, a man who was called just and devout, waiting for the coming of Messiah. It had been revealed to Simeon by the Holy Spirit that he

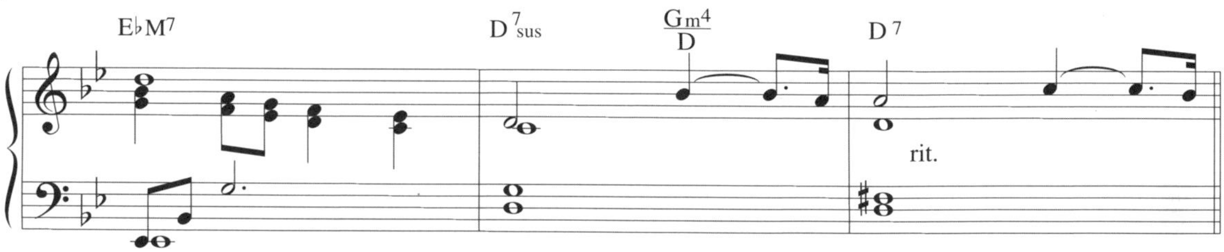

would not see death before he had seen the Lord's Christ. He was a man waiting in eager anticipation for the light of a new day.

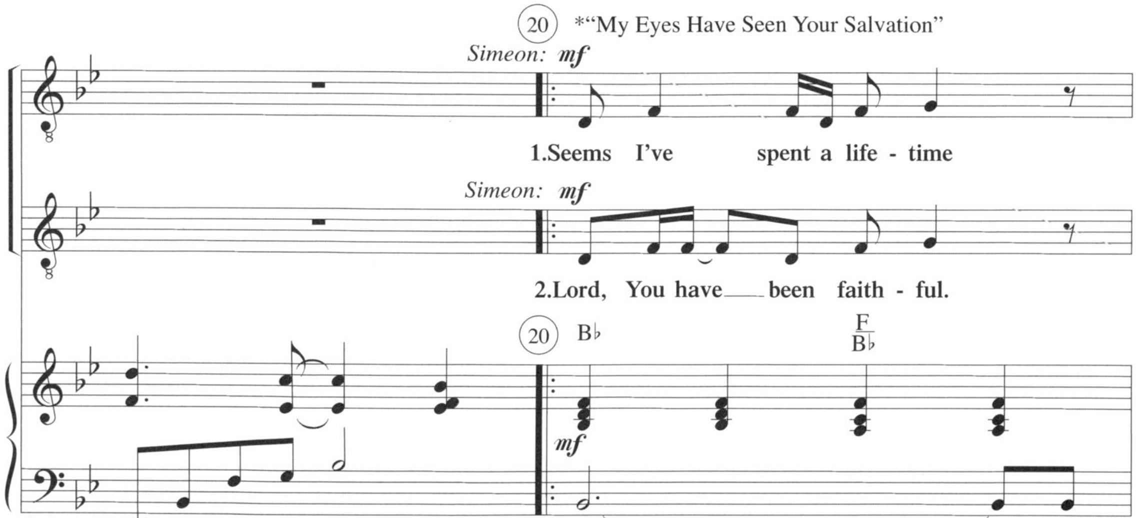

*Words and Music by Christopher Machen. Copyright © 1999 by Pilot Point Music (ASCAP). All rights reserved. Administered by The Copyright Company, 40 Music Square East, Nashville, TN 37203.

Wait - ing for this mo - ment to ar - rive.
How can I re - pay You for Your grace?
Eb/Bb
Ebm6/Bb
Bb
Eb2
(♮)
23
Joseph:
mf
There were times I won - dered If my faith was strong e - nough
Joseph:
mf
Heav - en holds my fu - ture For I have seen Sal - va - tion
23
Bb2
F/Bb
Eb/Bb
Ab9
slight rit.
Simeon:
26
A little faster ♩ = ca. 72
to sur - vive. But still I've trust - ed You, You've
Simeon:
face to face. I'll fall down to my knees, And
Dm7
Gm7
26
Eb
slight rit.
A little faster

Both
never let me down, Your Promise has come true, For the
Both
raise my voice to sing. With every breath in me, I will
F/E♭
Dm7
CD: 49 1st time
CD: 51 2nd time
cresc.
accel.
Savior I have found.
cresc.
accel.
worship Christ the King.
Gm7
Fsus F E♭/F
cresc.
accel.
31
Faster ♩ = ca. 78
Both f
My eyes have seen Your sal-
B♭
Cm7/F
f

35
va - tion. For what God has
E♭/B♭ B♭ B♭2 B♭ F/A Gm
prom - ised He has done. My
B♭/F C/E Cm7/F
39
eyes have seen Your Sal - va -
B♭ F/A F/G
43
rit. 1st time only
tion; For I've seen Je - sus Christ, God's
G Cm7 B♭/D Cm7/E♭ E♭/F
rit. 1st time only

1 Slower ♩ = ca. 66
47
CD: 50
Son.
B♭2
E♭M7
B♭2
Slower
(to pg. 85, meas. 20)
2
CD: 52
cresc. and accel.
Son.
E♭M7
B♭sus
B♭
B♭/A
cresc. and accel.
Faster ♩ = ca. 82
51
Joseph: f
You are the glo - ry for Your ho - ly na - tion.
Choir
f
Ah,
f
51
Gm
D/F♯
D+/F♯
D/F♯
Faster

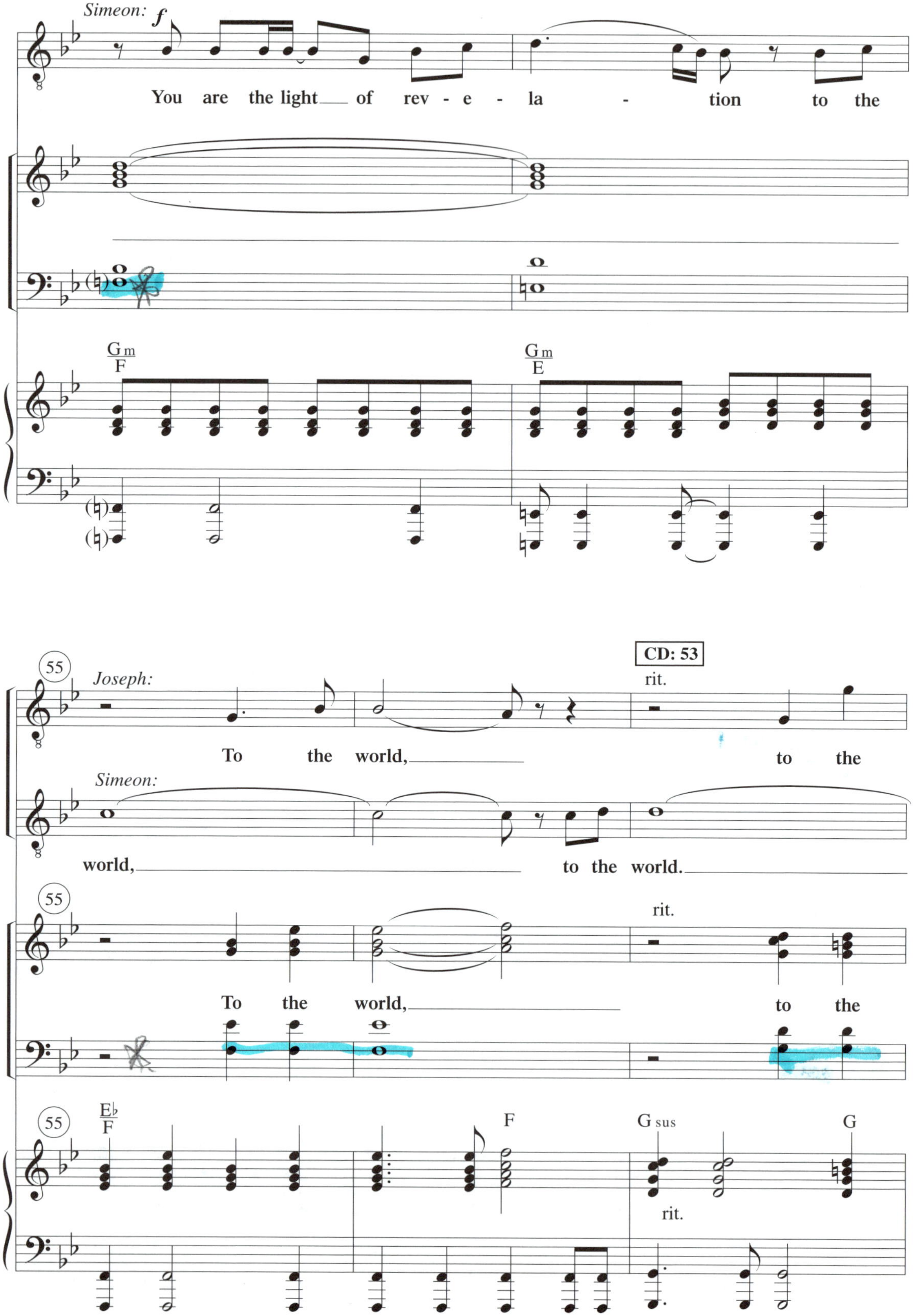
Simeon:
f
You are the light of rev - e - la - tion to the
Gm/F
Gm/E
55
Joseph:
To the world,
CD: 53
rit.
to the
Simeon:
world,
to the world.
To the world,
to the
Eb/F
F
Gsus
G
rit.

59
Both
a tempo
world.
My eyes have
Dm/G
Em/G
C
seen Your sal - va - tion.
For what
Dm7/G
F/C
C2
G/B

CD: 54
63
God has prom-ised He has done.
cresc.
Our God has prom - ised, He has
cresc.
Am C/G D/F♯
rit.
Joseph: ff
67
a tempo
My eyes have seen Your sal -
Simeon: ff
My eyes have seen Your sal -
done.
My eyes have seen Your sal -
ff
Dm/G F/G D♭ A♭/C
ff a tempo

cresc.
71
va - tion, I've seen
cresc.
va - tion, For I've seen Je - sus,
71
va - tion,
A♭/B♭
B♭
71
E♭m7
Je - sus, I've seen Je - sus,
I've seen Je - sus, I've seen
For I've seen Je - sus. For I've seen
E♭m7
E♭m/D♭
G♭/C♭
C♭M7
E♭m/B♭

75
rit.
Je - sus Christ, God's Son,
Je - sus Christ, God's Son,
75
rit.
Je - sus, God's Son,
G♭/A♭ A♭ B♭m/A♭ G♭/A♭ D♭ E♭/D♭
75
rit.
79
(6)
God's Son!
God's Son!
79
God's Son!
E/D♭ G♭/D♭ A♭/D♭ N.C. A/B B/A A/A♭ G♭m6 D♭
79
(♮)
8vb

Part VIII

JOURNEY OF PRAISE

includes

Angels, from the Realms of Glory
Bless That Wonderful Name
Wonderful Counselor
Jesus, O What a Wonderful Child

*"Angels, from the Realms of Glory"

Arranged by Camp Kirkland and Tom Fettke

*Music by Henry T. Smart. Arr. © 1999 by Pilot Point Music (ASCAP). All rights reserved. Administered by The Copyright Company, 40 Music Square East, Nashville, TN 37203.
**Words, Traditional and Ken Bible; Music, Traditional. Copyright © 1998, and this arr. © 1999 by Pilot Point Music (ASCAP). All rights reserved. Administered by The Copyright Company, 40 Music Square East, Nashville, TN 37203.
***If a trio is used, the alto part may be sung by a female or male (1st tenor).

of Je - sus.
of Je - sus.
E♭ A♭/E♭ E♭ Fm/E♭ E♭ E♭7/G
13
Bless that won-der-ful name of Je -
Ho - ly is the name of Je -
13
A♭ A♭7
17
sus. Bless that won-der-ful name of
sus. Ho - ly is the name of
E♭ Fm/E♭ E♭
17
A♭/B♭ E♭ A♭/E♭

21
Je - sus–
Je - sus–
No oth - er name
E♭/B♭ G/B G7/B Cm A♭m6/C♭
21
E♭/B♭ Cm7 F7
CD: 56 1st time
1
know.
(to pg. 95, meas. 9)
I know, name I know.
F7 B♭7 E♭ A♭7 E♭ A♭/B♭
2
know.
CD: 57
27
Swing ♩= ca. 122 f
Know, name I know.
2. Holy is the Name
E♭ A♭7 E♭ B♭m6/D♭ F/C F/A B♭ Dm/B
f Swing eighths

*Words and Music, Traditional. Arr. © 1999 by Pilot Point Music (ASCAP). All rights reserved. Administered by The Copyright Company, 40 Music Square East, Nashville, TN 37203.

37
new-born King. Well, I call Je - sus the Won-der-ful Coun - se-lor?
F/C C7 F C13
37
F
B♭/F F B♭/F F
41
Oh, oh, oh, oh, glo-ry hal-le-lu-jah. Oh, oh, oh, oh,
B♭9
F B♭/F F
41
B♭9
CD: 58
1st time
2nd time to Coda
forward to 102
Unison mf
glo-ry hal-le-lu-jah. Glo-ry hal-le-lu-jah to the new-born King. The
2nd time to Coda
F B♭/F F
F/A B♭ Dm/B
F/C C7 F F9/6

45
shep - herds wor - shipped a ba - by in a man - ger.
Oh, oh, oh, oh,
Unison mf
B♭9
glo - ry hal - le - lu - jah.
Divisi
49
The Ba - by Je - sus is the Won - der - ful Coun - sel - or.
F
B♭/F
F
B♭9
Oh, oh, oh, oh,
Unison
glo - ry hal - le - lu - jah.
Divisi
53
There were three wise men

look-in' for a Sav - ior.
They
Oh, oh, oh, oh,
glo-ry hal-le-lu-jah.
Unison
Divisi
B♭9
F
B♭/F
F
57
fol-lowed the star and it
led them to Beth - le-hem.
Oh, oh, oh, oh,
Unison
57
B♭9
CD: 59
61
Divisi
D.S. al Coda
Unison f
glo-ry hal-le-lu-jah.
Glo-ry hal-le-lu-jah to the new-born King.
Tell me
Divisi
Unison f
D.S. al Coda
F
B♭/F
F
61
F/A
B♭
Dm/B
F/C
C7
F
C13

CODA
64
new - born King.
Glo - ry hal - le - lu - jah to the new - born King.
CODA
F/C C7 F B♭/C
64
F F/A B♭ Dm/B F/C C7 F B♭/C
CD: 60
Same tempo ♩ = ca. 122
68
Straight eighths
Glo - ry hal - le - lu - jah to the new - born King.
F F/A B♭ Dm/B F/C C7
68
F
Straight eighths
70
f
Might - y is the name of
B♭/F
70
F B♭/C F B♭/F

74
Je - sus. Might - y is the name
F Gm/F F F7/A 74 B♭
of Je - sus.
B♭ B♭7 F Gm/F F B♭/C
78
Might - y is the name of Je -
78 F B♭/C F B♭/F F A/E A7/E

82
sus–
No oth - er name
I
Dm
B♭m6/D♭
F6/C
Dm7
G7
C7
Gospel shuffle, same tempo
86
♩ = ca. 122
know.
know, name I know.
F
B♭7
F
Cm/A
B♭
Swing eighths
CD: 61
B♭
B♭/A♭
G
Dm/B
C
C/D

*"Jesus, O What a Wonderful Child"

94
Je - sus, Je - sus, So low - ly,
Je - sus, Je - sus, So low - ly, meek and
94 G B 7♯5 3 Em7 A 7
98
meek and mild. New life, new hope, new
mild. New life, new hope, new
Em/D D 7 C/D 98 G Am/G

joy He brings; Won't you lis - ten to the
joy He brings; Won't you lis - ten to the
G Am G7/B C
102
CD: 62 1st time
2nd time to Coda (to pg. 111, meas. 122)
an - gels sing. Glo - ry, glo - ry, glo - ry to the
an - gels sing. Glo - ry, glo - ry, glo - ry to the
C#°7 G/D D/C G/B Am G#°7 Am/C

Solo
mf
106
Well, He was prom-ised by the
new - born King.
A7♭9 D7♯5 C/D G C/G G Bb/D
mf
proph-ets, The Hope of all the a - ges. Sweet
Am/G G C7 G Am/G G Am/G

110
Mar - y was His low - ly moth - er; The
mf
Oo
mf
G
B 7♯5
Em7
110
Ho - ly Spir - it was His Fa - ther. O the
Unison
He was His Fa - ther.
Tenors only
A9
D9 E♭9 E9 F9 F♯9

114
wise - men came from a - far, Guid - ed
Came from a - far,
Add basses Divisi
114
G9
on - ly by a shin - ing star. They
Oo, ah,
C7
F9

118
cresc.
CD: 63
found Him, they wor-shipped, They praised Him, my
118
G/D D/C G/B Am7 G#°7 Am/C
cresc.
D.S. al Coda
Je - sus, the Son of God. new - born King.
f
Woh, new - born King.
A7♭9 D7♯5 C/D G Am/G G A7♭9 D7♯5 C/D G

124
Glo - ry, glo - ry, glo - ry to the
Glo - ry, glo - ry, glo - ry to the
G
124
G/D
D/C
G/B
Am
G♯°7
Am/C
CD: 64
Straight eighths
accel.
new - born King.
Straight eighths
accel.
new - born King.
A7♭9
D7♯5
C/D
G
Straight eighths
accel.
C/D

129
f Faster ♩ = ca. 130
Praise that won - der - ful name of
f
129
G C/D G C/G
f Faster
Je - sus.
133
Praise that won-der-ful name
G Am/G G G7/B 133 C
of Je - sus.
C C7 G Am/G G C/D

137
Praise that won-der-ful name of Je -
137
G C/D G C/G G B/F♯ B7/F♯
sus–
141
CD: 65
No oth-er-name I
Em Cm6/E♭ 141 G6/D Em7 A7 D7
know.
know, name I know.
G C7 G E♭7

145
ff
Bless that won-der-ful name of Je -
A♭ D♭/E♭ A♭ D♭/A♭ A♭
sus. Bless that won-der-ful name of
149
A♭ B♭m/A♭ A♭ A♭7/C D♭
Je - sus. Bless that won-der-ful name
153
D♭7 A♭ B♭m/A♭ A♭ D♭/E♭ A♭ D♭/E♭ A♭

of
Je - sus–
A♭
D♭/A♭
C/G
F m
D♭m6/F♭
157
No oth - er name
I,
A♭6/E♭
F m7
B♭7
E♭7
161
I

know. Bless that won - der - ful, won - der - ful,
A♭
D♭/E♭
165
won - der - ful, won - der - ful name.
165
D♭/E♭
A♭
great rit.
His name is Je - sus!
D♭9
great rit.
A♭

Part IX

JOURNEY TO OUR HEARTS

includes

Thou Didst Leave Thy Throne

Down to Earth

Arranged by Camp Kirkland and Tom Fettke

*Words by Emily E. S. Elliott; Music by Timothy R. Matthews. Arr.

**Words and Music by Kevin Stokes and Pete Carlson.

an - gels sang in joy - ous praise to the won - der born that night. He whom
gift that God had of - fered was the heart and soul of love. In His
A/B G2 D2/F♯ A
10
proph - ets had fore - told had fi - nal - ly ar - rived, The
smile we saw Heav - en, the face of God Him - self. For-
10
Gm7 B♭/C C7 F F4/2 F F/A
CD: 67 1st time
CD: 69 2nd time
cresc.
prom - ise of Mes - si - ah, love brought to life.
cresc.
ev - er met the pres - ent who we've come to know our - selves.
B♭2 Gm7 Em7
cresc.

Both times
mf
15
He came down to earth, to this world a tin - y ba - by; A liv-ing
Choir or Ensemble
mp
Oo
mp
G/A A7 A13 A7 D2 DM7 Em7/D
mf
Sav - ior in a man - ger far a - way. He came
Bm2 Bm/A G2 D2/F♯

19
down to earth, breaking thro' all time to reach us, And
Oo
19
Em7 Em7/A A7 F♯7/A♯ B4/2 Bm Bm/A
still He's reach - ing out for us to - day. This lit - tle
E9/G♯ A sus A7

23
Child was this glo-rious King we cel-e-brate on Christ-mas eve; He came
Oo
G2 G F♯sus F♯7♭9 B4/2 Bm/A G2 D2/F♯
26
CD: 70 2nd time
1
down to earth, down to you and me.
Em7 D/F♯ G2 G6/A A7 D2

CD: 68
(to pg. 118, meas. 6)
mp
2
2.It was down to you and me.
D/C G/B B♭+ Em7/B♭ Bm9
(to pg. 118, meas. 6)
2
G2 G6/A A7
33
O the mir - a - cle so time - less en - tered
D2 D
33
Am7 C/D D7

CD: 71
in a world of night, And ev - ery prayer was an - swered by this
G2 D2/F♯ Em7 F♯m7 Bm7 Bm
ho - ly Child of light. He came
D/A Asus G/A A9 B♭13 B♭7

38
down to earth, to this world a tin - y ba - by; A liv-ing
Oo
38
E♭2
E♭M7
Fm7/E♭
Sav-ior in a man-ger far a-way. He came down to earth, break-ing
42
Oo
Cm7
Cm/B♭
A♭2
E♭/G
42
Fm7
Fm7/B♭
B♭7

thro' all time to reach us, And still He's reach - ing out for us to -
G7/B C4 2 Cm Cm/B♭ F7/A
46
day. This lit-tle Child was this glo-rious King we cel - e - brate on
B♭sus B♭7 46 A♭2 A♭ G sus G7 C4 2 Cm/B♭

50
Christ-mas eve; He came down to earth,
Oo Oo
A♭2 E♭2/G Fm7 E♭/G A♭2 E♭/G
CD: 72
rit.
down to you and me.
Fm7 B♭sus B♭ E♭2 E♭ E♭7 A♭/E♭ E♭+ A♭m6/E♭

INVITATION OPPORTUNITY: Although it is optional, we hope everyone will elect to use this moment in the musical for spiritual renewal and outreach.

Part X

THE JOURNEY CONTINUES

includes

Joy to the World

The Lord Will Come Again

Arranged by Camp Kirkland and Tom Fettke

*Music by George Frederick Handel. Arr. © 1999 by Pilot Point Music (ASCAP). All rights reserved. Administered by The Copyright Company, 40 Music Square East, Nashville, TN 37203.

1st time: Choir unison
2nd time: Ladies unison
mf
17
*"The Lord Will Come Again"
1.We lift our eyes from Beth - le - hem to
(2.As the) cen - tu - ries pass quick - ly by the
Ladies
B♭ F B♭ E♭2 F/A
mf
see the set - ting sun, Our
time is draw - ing near. With
Both times: All
E♭/G F/A F/B♭ B♭ F/B♭ B♭ F/B♭ B♭
22
Divisi
hearts cry "Mar - a - nath - a, Lord Je - sus, quick - ly
proph - e - cies pre - dict - ing that soon He will ap -
Divisi
22
D♭ E♭/D♭ A♭/C G♭/B♭ A♭/C

Unison
26
come." We wor - ship and a - dore you, Lord, we
pear. Let an - gels fill the skies a - gain, O
Unison
B♭/D
E♭2
F/A
30
Divisi
long to see Your face. So let Your
let your glo - ries ring. This Child of
Divisi
E♭/G
F/A
F/B♭
B♭
F/B♭
B♭
B♭M7/D
ra - di - ance fill all the heav - ens,
Beth - le - hem, born in a man - ger
E♭
B♭
B♭M7/D
E♭
D

34
Unison
and let our praise pre - pare the
is now our soon and com - ing
Unison
D Bb BbM7/D Eb Am/C C9
CD: 75 1st time
CD: 77 2nd time
cresc.
way.
King.
cresc.
39
Divisi f
Joy to the world!
Divisi f
Ab Fsus F Bb F Bb
cresc.
f
the Lord is come, and He is com-ing a-gain.
Bb F/Bb Bb/D BbM7/D Eb Bb/D Bb/F F

43
Joy to the earth! the Sav - ior reigns For -
43
B♭ F B♭ B♭/D E♭ Gm/E Fsus F
ev - er and ev - er the king - dom of this world is be - come the
47
B♭ F B♭ F B♭ E♭ B♭ F Gm F B♭ F/A
3
king - dom of our Lord, Shout with joy to the world!
51
Gm F/A G/B F/A G/B Cm7 F/A B♭/A♭

Unison
the Lord will come a - gain!
Unison
B♭/A♭ E♭/G E♭M7/G F sus F
1 B♭ F/B♭ B♭
CD: 76
56
D.S.
Unison mf
Ladies
2.As the
E♭/B♭ F/B♭ B♭
F/B♭ B♭
E♭/B♭ F/B♭ B♭
2
gain.
CD: 78
E♭2/G B♭2/F E♭2
mf

62
mf
Divisi
Unison
All You have made will
praise You, O Lord;
66
All You have
mf
made will ex - tol You.
Divisi
Divisi
And the
B♭2/D
E♭2/G
F/A
B♭sus
B♭
E♭2/G
F/A
E♭/B♭
B♭
F/A

70
glo - r'ous splen - dor of Your king - dom,
The glo - r'ous
70
Gm
Dm7
E♭M7
The glo - r'ous splen - dor of Your
splen - dor of Your king - dom, The
74
F2
74
Gm
Dm7
king - dom, The glo - r'ous
glo - r'ous splen - dor of Your king - dom,
78
E♭M7
F2
78
Gm

splen - dor of Your king - dom.
of Your king - dom.
Dm7
E♭M7
F2
82
All You have made will praise You,
E♭2/G
F/A
E♭/B♭
B♭
CD: 79
cresc.
O Lord!
B♭
Fm/A♭
G sus
G

88
f
Joy to the world! the Lord is come, And He is
C G C G/C C/E CM7/E F C/E
coming again.
92
Joy to the earth! the Savior
C/G G C G C C/E F Am/F♯
reigns For-ever and ever the kingdom of this
Gsus G C G C G C
96
F C

world is be - come the king - dom of our Lord. Shout with
G Am G C G/B Am G/B A/C♯ G/B A/C♯
100
CD: 80
joy to the world! the Lord will come,
Dm7 G/B C/B♭ F/A FM7/A G sus
104
Shout with joy to the world! the Lord will
G G/B A/C♯ Dm7 G/B C/B♭ F/A FM7/A

108
come!
Shout with joy to the world!
G sus
G
G/B
A/C♯
D m7
G/B
C/B♭
the Lord will come
Unison
a - gain,
a - gain,
C/B♭
F/A
F M7/A
G sus
G
112
F C F C
F C F C
F C F C

116
a - gain!
He will come a -
F C F
F C F C
F C F C F C F
Divisi
gain!
Divisi
C G/C C C/B♭
A♭ Gm7 Fm7 Gm7 Fm7 B♭
C
8vb

PASTORAL CONCLUSION: The theme of *Journey of Hope* is a great set-up for the new millennium. As we face an unknown future, There is Hope! That hope is communicated clearly in this work, with passion and power. Thus after "The Lord Will Come Again", you may wish your Pastor to conclude the presentation with a few words of encouragement. The benediction, "There is Hope" would follow. If the Pastor utilized the "Invitation Opportunity" for his short closing message you may wish to end the presentation in a bright and triumphant mood. Thus,"The Lord Will Come Again" would be the last selection. Or, go directly to "There is Hope" after "The Lord Will Come Again" (or after a closing prayer).

There Is Hope

Benediction

Words and Music by
CHRISTOPHER MACHEN
Arranged by Camp Kirkland
and Tom Fettke

With expectation ♩ = ca. 63

8
heart, shin - ing on the soul, forc - ing back the
C2/E FM7 G G♯°7 E7/G♯
dark to re - veal the light of Hope gives our spir - its
11
Divisi
cresc. poco a poco
Am Dm7 Gsus G C CM7 Dm/C C
peace, peace breaks forth in praise for the prom - ised
Gsus G G/F C2/E C/E C/G FM7

15
King for His gift of grace, God's most Ho - ly
G Em7 E7sus Em7 FM7 Dm7 Dm6 Dm7
One, Yet our hearts cry out 'til Mes - si - ah
E7 E7♯5 E7 Am FM7 F6 FM7
f
19
comes. We be - lieve tho' we face de - spair. For
Gsus G/F C2/E C/E F C G/B Am Fm6/A♭

CD: 82
still there is hope.
C/G
G sus
G
C
A♭/C
24
Unison
mf
Hope ech - oes thro' the day, Thro' a fer - vent
D♭
G♭/D♭
D♭
A♭sus
A♭
A♭/G♭
prayer, voic - es speak from faith, wor - ship fills the
27
D♭2/F
D♭/F
G♭M7
A♭
F7♭9/A
F7/A

30
Divisi
air. God re-veals His love and Hope gives our spir-its
Divisi
B♭m E♭m7 A♭sus A♭ 30 D♭ D♭M7 E♭m/D♭ D♭
cresc. poco a poco
peace, peace breaks forth in praise for the Prom-ised
cresc. poco a poco
A♭sus A♭ A♭/G♭ D♭2/F D♭/F D♭/A♭ G♭M7
cresc. poco a poco
34
King, for His gift of grace, God's most Ho-ly
34
A♭ Fm7 F7sus Fm7 G♭M7 E♭m7 E♭m6 E♭m7

One. Yet our hearts cry out 'til Mes - si - ah
F7 F7♯5 F7 B♭m G♭M7 G♭6 G♭M7
CD: 83
ff rit.
comes.
39
Unison
f a tempo
Hope gives our spir-its
A♭sus A♭ B♭sus B♭ E♭ A♭/E♭ E♭
cresc. poco a poco
peace, peace breaks forth in praise for the Prom - ised
B♭sus B♭ B♭/A♭ E♭/G E♭/B♭ A♭M7

42
Divisi
King, for His gift of grace, God's most Ho - ly
Divisi
B♭ Gm7 G7sus Gm7 A♭M7 Fm7 Fm6 Fm7
44
One. Yet our hearts cry out 'til Mes - si - ah
G7 G7♯5 G7 Cm A♭M7 A♭6 A♭M7
ff
comes.
48
f
We be-lieve,
B♭sus
B♭/A♭
E♭2/G E♭/G A♭

decresc.
tho' we face de - spair. For still there is hope, for
mf
Eb
Bb/D
Cm
Abm6/Cb
Eb/Bb
F/A
52
rit. e decresc.
still there is hope,
mp
Still there is
Abm
Abm6
Eb2/G
Eb/G
Fm7/4
Bb7sus
Bb7
mf rit. e decresc.
hope.
hope.
Eb

JOURNEY of HOPE THE BIRTH of THE SAVIOR

JOURNEY of HOPE THE BIRTH of THE SAVIOR

JOURNEY of HOPE THE BIRTH of THE SAVIOR

A MUSICAL BY

Camp Kirkland & Tom Fettke

JOURNEY of HOPE THE BIRTH of THE SAVIOR

JOURNEY of HOPE THE BIRTH of THE SAVIOR

JOURNEY of HOPE THE BIRTH of THE SAVIOR

Journey of Hope

The Birth of the Savior

Journey of Hope
The Birth of the Savior
Journey of Hope
The Birth of the Savior
Journey of Hope
The Birth of the Savior

A MUSICAL BY

Camp Kirkland & Tom Fettke